The Child Within

Danell Coleman

This book is dedicated to:

Jesus: The One True God; The Author and Finisher of our faith; our Father, Healer, Friend, Redeemer, Lover of our soul, and Savior. You have made me, kept me, healed me, loved me, directed my path, and blessed me abundantly. I am sorry for the many times that I did not exemplify You, yet, You loved me and cared for me. I love you with all my heart!

My wonderful gift from God - my loving husband. You have quietly endured many of my emotional battles, of which I'm sure you prayed about more times than I know. I am sorry, but I thank you for loving me through it all! I can't believe it's been 30 years since we said "I do"... twice, but I'd do it all over again because I know YOU are the one God had for me. I love you times a googolplex!

My two greatest blessings - Josh and Tash! I prayed all of your life that my emotional baggage would not leave a scar on you. I am so sorry for the times that I was not who I should have been for you and I hope that you can forgive, but mostly forget. You are the best human beings on this planet and you make us so proud for being just who you are. I love you so much!

My trainers, prayer warriors, and overall supporters - my parents. You saw me through most of this journey while going through your own struggles. Thank you for not giving up on me and loving me through it all. I'm sorry for the pain and embarrassment that I caused you, but I know your forgiving hearts and I love and appreciate you for that. My heart is saddened, Dad, that you did not get a chance to read this before passing. Less than two months after writing this dedication, I never dreamed you'd be gone that soon. I love and miss you so much!

To anyone that I have hurt physically or emotionally - I am truly sorry and I ask for your forgiveness! God has healed me and my prayer for everyone is that if you have not accepted Jesus as your Healer and/or Savior, that you please do so soon. Our time on this earth is coming to an end and the Bible says "As it was in the days of Noah, so it will be at the coming of the Son of Man" (Matthew 24:37 NIV). Don't be like the people in Noah's time, laughing and jeering at the Christians, instead of heeding our pleas to turn it all over to Jesus. The hurts, the sorrow, the disappointment, the sickness, the pain, the turmoil, the broken life. Allow Him to be your Healer, Peacemaker, Friend, Father, and Savior. I love you with the love of Jesus!

Contents

Acknowledgements

I would like to express my sincere gratitude to the following individuals who have supported and encouraged me throughout the writing of this book:

* First and foremost, I thank Jesus Christ for giving me the words to write my story and for all the blessings He has bestowed upon me.
* My wonderful and loving husband, Dean-Andrew Coleman, for his unwavering support and belief in me. Thank you for reading, suggesting, and helping me navigate the publishing process.
* My mother, Arlene Speakman, for her meticulous proofreading, encouragement, and for all that you have poured into my life.
* Denise Porter, for diligently proofreading and correcting my rough draft. Your dedication to teaching has been an inspiration to our blessings which resulted in you becoming one of their favorite teachers!
* David Bowman, for the beautiful artwork that you have permitted me to use for the cover. I searched many pieces and as soon as I saw "Security" my breath stopped and I knew that was the one! It is so aptly named.

Without the support of these individuals, this book would not have been possible. I am truly grateful for their contributions.

Preface

This book began as what I thought to be children's stories. But as I kept reading over them, I just felt that they were a little heavy for children, even though I had tried to "tone them down." As I was reading the book that my sister wrote and just published, the thought came to me that maybe they are stories for the child that is still in us, and that is how I was able to complete "The Confused Little Girl" story. I then decided to turn the stories into a 7-day devotion, however, I needed one more story. I thought about it for a week, I knew that I wanted to talk about being made fun of, but I didn't know what emotion to use. Tonight, as I was reading another book, the word embarrassed popped into my mind and I knew I had my final story. So, with that in mind, I will begin each chapter with my "Little Girl" stories and then expound upon them as the Lord directs.

May Jesus speak to the "Little Child" inside you, who needs to be healed and accept the Father's love. For you are "fearfully and wonderfully made!"

1. The Sad Little Girl

Once upon a time, there lived a very happy little girl. She loved her family very much and they loved her.

The happy little girl lived on a farm with her mommy, daddy, and older brother. Her Grandma and Grandpa lived on another farm just down the road, and she would visit them almost every day.

The happy little girl loved living on a farm. There were tractors, trucks, combines, big cows, stinky pigs, and mean chickens (well, she thought they were mean because they would peck her when she helped gather eggs). Best of all she loved "helping" her daddy and grandpa and just being with them made her happy.

One night the happy little girl's mommy and daddy were yelling at each other. She didn't know why this was happening, but it scared her, so she hid under the table with her big brother.

The mommy hurt the little girl's daddy and he began to cry; this made the little girl sad and she began to cry. The happy little girl was now a sad little girl.

One day the sad little girl moved in with her grandparents and her mommy moved to another house. She liked living with her grandma and grandpa, especially because she would see her daddy every day.

The sad little girl liked to help her grandma make big delicious meals for her daddy and grandpa. This taught her how to cook and gave her a passion for it as an adult.

When the sad little girl was eight years old, her mommy decided to move far away. This made the sad little girl even more sad. Her daddy, new mommy, and grandparents would pray for her every day. Eventually, Jesus took the sadness and helped her to become a happy little girl once again.

Happy or Sad?

...

Have you ever noticed how easy it is for a child to show his or her emotions? I was in a restaurant yesterday talking to my husband and best friend when I noticed the cute little boy sitting three tables away from us. There was no one sitting between us, so I had a clear view of him. I later found out that the man he was sitting with was his uncle. In the span of 15 minutes, he went from happy to tears and back to happy again. His sad period only lasted a couple of minutes and during that moment he had his uncle and three employees attend to him. There's something about a crying toddler, especially a cute one, that attracts the attention of the adults around them.

In the Sermon on the Mountain in Matthew 5, Jesus said, "Blessed are those who mourn, for they will be comforted." This is a promise. When we cry out to the Lord, how much more does He want to attend to us? His love for us is unconditional, it is never-ending, He loves us far more than we can comprehend with our human minds. In Matthew 11:28 He says, "Come to me, all you who are weary and burdened, and I will give you rest." Verse 29 goes on to say "…, for I am gentle and humble in heart, and you will find rest for your souls" (NIV).

During one of my sad periods as an adult, this song became popular as a worship song. May it minister to you as much as it did to me during that time.

The more I seek you
The more I find you
The more I find you, the more I love you
I wanna sit at your feet
Drink from the cup in your hand
Lay back against you and breathe, feel your heartbeat
This love is so deep, it's more than I can stand
I melt in your peace, it's overwhelming

Song by Gateway Worship and Kari Jobe / Songwriters: Zach Neese / The More I Seek You lyrics © Capitol CMG Publishing, Integrity Music

Sometimes we just need to "sit at His feet ... and breathe." The way we do this is by reading His Word, praying, singing worship songs, and waiting for Him to speak to us. Soon His peace will come and overwhelm you.

Notes

_____

_____

_____

_____

_____

_____

_____

_____

2. The Shy Little Girl

Once upon a time, there lived a shy little girl who did not like it when grown-ups talked to her, especially if they expected her to answer their questions.

One Sunday at church, a big adult asked the shy little girl a question. She was so shy that she ran and hid behind her grandma.

The next Sunday the shy little girl saw her daddy talking to the pastor so she ran up to him, grabbed him by the leg, and squeezed as tight as she could. She knew her daddy would be so happy that she was giving him a hug so she looked up at him expecting to see him smiling down at her. However, when she looked up it wasn't her daddy, it was the pastor who was looking down at her! Once again she ran and hid behind her grandma.

At Christmas time every year, the Sunday school children would stand in front of the congregation, quote a verse, and sing a song. The shy little girl did not want to do this but all of the adults insisted. When it was her turn, she stepped just a little too close to the microphone and her mouth touched it sending a shock through her lips...and laughter through the congregation. This time she could not hide so she just stood there and cried.

When the shy little girl was six years old, she got a new mommy. At first, she didn't like the new mommy and wouldn't talk to her; but after a while, she began to realize what a good person the new mommy was, and eventually, she began to love her.

God knew that the new mommy was exactly who the shy little girl needed in her life to help her overcome her shyness. As time moved on and the shy little girl got older, the shyness faded away and confidence took its place.

Shyness or Just Another Form of Fear?

...

Why did I want to run and hide when I was a child? Because I was afraid of people that were bigger than me or a stranger to me. I think that by the time most people become adults they overcome their shyness or at least the fear of interacting with other people, but those feelings can still be there and pop out at any moment. I am a very short adult and I still have times when I am intimidated by people who are taller than me, which isn't saying much considering my 5 foot ½ inch stature.

There are some things that we have to work at, as Christians, and some things the Lord just gives us. Overcoming shyness may be one of those things you have to work at; however, He will give you the ability and strength to overcome.

Moses was shy, he begged the Lord not to send him to Egypt. Exodus 4:10-12 ESV: "But Moses said to the Lord, 'Oh, my Lord, I am not eloquent, either in the past or since you have spoken to your servant, but I am slow of speech and of tongue.' Then the Lord said to him, 'Who has made man's mouth? Who makes him mute, or deaf, or seeing, or blind? Is it not I, the Lord? Now therefore go, and I will be with your mouth and teach you what you shall speak.'" So, Moses went, believing that God would be with him and give him the words to speak. Thankfully we know the story and we know that God did follow through on His promise, and He will follow through for you as well. Pray and ask God to give you the words to speak, to think clearly, and to have peace of mind and a restful spirit.

The Lord "fearfully and wonderfully made" you (Psalm 139:14), He knows exactly what you are like and He knows exactly what He created you for. The New Living Translation of this verse states, "Thank you for making me so wonderfully complex! Your workmanship is marvelous - how well I know it." Only God can make something so wonderfully complex and that thing He made is YOU!

Philippians 4 has many nuggets to help shy people, such as verses 6-8: "Do not be anxious about anything, but in every situation, by prayer and petition, with thanksgiving, present your requests to God. And the peace of God, which transcends all understanding, will guard your hearts and your minds in Christ Jesus. Finally, brothers and sisters, whatever is true, whatever is noble, whatever is right, whatever is pure, whatever is lovely, whatever is admirable - if anything is excellent or praiseworthy - think about such things." (NIV).

Every day quote Philippians 4:13: "I can do all things through Christ who strengthens me" (NKJV).

He will give you the boldness you need for every encounter, every thought you want to share, every phone call you need to make, EVERY situation you find yourself in, where your shyness wants to keep you hidden.

Notes

3. The Mad Little Girl

Once upon a time, there lived a mad little girl.

She was mad because she felt that the people she loved had hurt her. The mad little girl's mommy hurt her because she moved to another house and now they were no longer a family. After a couple of years, the mad little girl's daddy hurt her because he brought a strange lady around and he was paying more attention to her than the little girl.

One day the daddy said he was going to marry the strange lady. This made the mad little girl really mad, mostly at the lady, so she decided not to talk to the strange lady anymore even though she was going to be her new mommy.

Jesus helped the mad little girl to realize what a good person the new mommy was and the mad little girl began to love the new mommy.

But the mad little girl was still angry about other things that had happened to her, like her real mommy moving far away, and kids making fun of her at school. So, she would lash out at people with mean words or even hit them.

The mad little girl became a confused teenager who struggled with many different emotions, but God was patient with her, and one by one He helped the mad little girl until one day she realized that she was no longer mad.

"Don't be Mad, Get Glad"

...

Boy is that easier said than done! Anger was a part of my life for many years, long into my adulthood. Thankfully I did stop hitting people, believe me, the urge was still there! I did find myself smacking the table or desk so hard that it not only scared the people around me but it scared me too, not to mention the pain in my hand.

As I moved through my adulthood, that quick anger toward others turned to anger toward myself, leading to self-hatred. In Psalm 37 the Bible says, "Refrain from anger and turn from wrath; do not fret - it leads only to evil. For those who are evil will be destroyed, but those who hope in the Lord will inherit the land" (NIV). Anger leads to evil. As a Christian no more needs to be said on the subject because we do not want to be led into evil, yet ... we still struggle with that stinking temper. I think the evil in my case was self-hatred; it kept me from pursuing some things that I felt the Lord calling me to do, and it came out in snappy little bitter quips to what other people felt was aimed at them.

A lot of my anger as a child stemmed from my biological mother; the way she treated my dad, her leaving our home and filing for divorce, then leaving Ohio and moving to Florida, the lifestyle that she lived which was the furthest from a Christian life one could get, and the list goes on. I remember one particular time after getting off the phone with her I was so angry, so I went to talk to my mom (you would know her as my step-mom). She told me the Bible says, "Be ... angry and sin not" (Ephesians 4:46 KJV). She reminded me that Jesus got angry in the temple, so angry that He turned the tables and seats over and even drove the people out (Matthew 21:12-13). I would venture to say that everyone probably gets angry at various times, however, for those of us who struggle with this spirit, it's how we express our anger that matters. This is another one of those emotions that we have to work on. I had to make a conscious effort to not hit, stomp my foot, or hit the table. As an adult, I had to stop and take a breath before responding to others, and for my self-hatred, I had to change my wording.

The Bible tells us to "Get rid of all bitterness, rage and anger, brawling and slander, along with every form of malice. Be kind and compassionate to one another, forgiving each other, just as in Christ God forgave you (Ephesians 4:31-32 NIV).

Notes

_____

_____

_____

_____

_____

_____

4. The Scared Little Girl

Once upon a time, there lived a scared little girl. She did not know why she became so afraid but afraid she was: of the dark, of being alone, of standing near a window at night, of the basement, of the attic, the list just seemed to go on and on.

The scared little girl lived in an old farmhouse which meant that her bedroom was upstairs and the bathroom was downstairs. Whenever she had to go to the bathroom during the night, she would have to turn on every light along the way. Going to the bathroom was better than going back to bed because that meant she had to turn the lights back off. So she would run up the stairs to escape the dark room behind her.

The scared little girl turned into a scared teenager. After years of being afraid, the scared teenager began to pray and ask Jesus to take the fear away. One night she had a dream that she was lying in bed and something was holding a blanket so tight over her that she couldn't move. Jesus came into the room and removed the blanket from her. When she woke up she realized that she was no longer afraid. Jesus gave her peace and assurance that He would always be with her.

The peaceful teenager remembered a dream she'd had years earlier when she was a little girl. In the dream, someone entered her room and pinned her under her blanket so tight that she couldn't move. For the rest of her life, the peaceful teenager has thanked Jesus for removing that blanket of fear from her.

The Spirit of Fear

...

"For God has not given us a spirit of fear, but of power and of love and of a sound mind" (II Tim 1:7 NKJV).

You can probably tell that these first few stories were the original ones I was going to use as my children's books. This is the story that I tried to "tame down" because the last thing I wanted to do was make a child scared. However, the truth of the story is, that dream that I had when I was younger, the "someone" was actually several demons holding the blanket down. In my dream, they had come into my room jeering and dancing around my bed then pinned me down. I do not know how old I was when I had the dream, but I do know that it was from that point on that I was consumed with fear until Jesus rescued me.

Fear is crippling, physically and mentally. It keeps us from venturing out, trying new things, enjoying life, and worst of all, it keeps us from simply living life. It can make you shake or cry uncontrollably or cause you to freeze, unable to move for hours. Fear takes on different aspects, depending on the person. You can be fearful of change, afraid of the dark, paranoid of health issues, or possess a phobia. It can vary in degrees, from keeping you from making a simple phone call to vomiting at just the thought of speaking in front of an audience. It can make you tip-toe into unknown territory or take off in a full sprint at an unfamiliar sound. It will keep some people in the same unfulfilling job for 40 years while others switch every year or so to keep from falling into a rut.

Whatever your fear, know that it is a trap from the enemy to keep you from fulfilling your purpose and calling. Give it to God, surrender to Him all of your anxieties, worries, nervousness, timidity, trepidation, distress, apprehensions … FEARS! One day you will wake up and realize that the crippling fear is gone!

In the meantime, continue to pray and read/quote scriptures such as the following:

1. "When I am afraid, I put my trust in You. In God, whose word I praise - in God I trust and am not afraid" (Psalm 56:3-4a NIV).
2. "Cast all your anxiety on him because he cares for you" (1 Peter 5:7 NIV).
3. "Be strong and courageous. Do not be afraid, do not be discouraged, for the Lord your God will be with you wherever you go" (Joshua 1:9b NIV).

Notes

_____

_____

_____

_____

5. The Embarrassed Little Girl

Once upon a time, there lived an embarrassed little girl. She was embarrassed about several things but mostly about her weight. Pudgy is what most people started out calling her, and as the embarrassed little girl got older, the word changed to fat. Kids at school made fun of her; they would choose her last to be on their team, or they just would not play with her at all.

The embarrassed little girl was uncomfortable about her clothes. Although she loved living on a farm, farmers were struggling at that time so there wasn't a lot of money. The little girl's mommy did the best she could by buying clothes at yard sales, but kids do not understand the struggles of adulthood so they get embarrassed about not having new or in-style clothes. The little girl was so embarrassed that she would wear her coat all day during school to hide the clothes she had on.

The embarrassed little girl was also ashamed of a lot of her behaviors. She would feel horrible after getting mad and hitting someone or yelling really loudly. She was embarrassed that she was too shy to talk to people, and they would just shrug their shoulders and walk away or start talking to someone else. She also felt embarrassed when someone would make her cry.

The embarrassed little girl became an embarrassed adult; every time she made a mistake she just wanted to hide. The embarrassed adult felt like all she did was make mistakes or make people mad or hurt their feelings when all she ever wanted to do was please people and make them happy.

One day, the embarrassed adult was given the opportunity to have surgery. She lost a lot of weight which helped her to feel better about herself. Now the adult has more confidence and belief in the talents God gave her and is more willing to pursue those talents. Also, because God healed the embarrassed adult of many emotions throughout her life, she does not have as many reasons to be embarrassed anymore.

We Are Just Human

...

"**I** trust in you, my God. Please do not let me be ashamed. Do not let my enemies laugh at me, because they are stronger than me" (Psalm 25:2 EEBV).

Let's face it, we all have been embarrassed at some point in our lives. Some people, like my husband and Mom, can get past it by making people laugh at something they say. For instance, one day as we were leaving a restaurant, Mom fell, right off the curb, instantly bringing an "Oooooh" from people waiting in line. We go back and help her up, she turns toward the people, shoots her hands in the air, and shouts, "I bet you didn't know you were going to get dinner AND a show!" "Make 'em laugh!" That's their motto. I, on the other hand, would jump up, NEVER look back, and make a beeline for the car, thanking the Lord that I never have to see those people again. Boy, I wish I could "make 'em laugh!"

I didn't like to have attention drawn to me, because I knew what people would think. Always negative, always condescending, always abhorring. That's what I told myself and I believed it. It didn't help that one of the many times I had lost weight, I was feeling so good about myself. I had this cute black and white outfit that I wore to the State Fair. A group of people about my age walked past me and one of the guys mooed like a cow. I was devastated.

Prayer works, as I have mentioned in the previous stories and I believe in miracles. However, there are some times that we just need to go to a doctor. He gave us doctors and He gave them the wisdom and mental capacity to learn. I am so thankful for my gastric bypass surgery and although I still need to lose about 40 pounds four years later, I no longer feel like every head turns and looks of disgust cross their faces.

Once again, we are "fearfully and wonderfully made." He created our emotions and our looks. Man and Satan have put into place the expectations that the world says we are to live up to or look like. If we degrade ourselves or others, we are degrading God's creation, His handiwork. We are just human, a creation, not perfect but perfectly made.

Allow God to speak to you through the words of Jeremiah. Take it to heart, as if God is speaking directly to you.

> "Then the word of the Lord came to me, saying: "Before I formed you in the womb I knew you; before you were born I sanctified you; I ordained you a prophet to the nations." Then said I: "Ah, Lord God! Behold, I cannot speak, for I am a youth." But the Lord said to me: "Do not say, 'I am a youth,' for you shall go to all to whom I send you, and whatever I command you, you shall speak. <u>Do not be afraid of their faces</u>, for I am with you to deliver you," says the Lord.

Then the Lord put forth His hand
and touched my mouth, and the
Lord said to me: "Behold, I have
put My words in your mouth"
(Jeremiah 1:4-9 NKJV).

Notes

_____

_____

_____

_____

_____

_____

6. The Confused Little Girl

Once upon a time, there lived a confused little girl. She was confused because she had so many different emotions in her that seemed to always show up when other people were around. Someone would hurt her feelings which made her cry and then someone else would say or do something that would make her mad so she would yell at them or even hit them. Sometimes strangers would talk to the confused little girl, and she had no idea what to say back to them; she just wanted to run and hide. But the worst feeling of all was the fear that seemed to hold her tight. It seemed like she was afraid of everything.

As the confused little girl got older, Jesus healed her of those emotions; however, other emotions seemed to take their place, such as worthlessness, embarrassment, loneliness, doubt, and self-denial. All of these led to self-hatred and she became a confused teenager and eventually a confused adult.

The confused adult could not understand how she could be a Christian, who loved Jesus with all of her heart and longed for nothing more than to be in His will and please Him, and still have all of these negative emotions and ill feelings toward herself. The thing that confused her the most was the Bible says the second commandment is to "love your neighbor as yourself," but she loved her neighbor and abhorred herself.

Jesus told the confused adult time and time again just how much He loved her. She accepted His love, but still could not bring herself to love the one she saw in the mirror. One day while she was looking in the mirror, the Lord told her to study every one of her features very carefully. The confused adult did. She looked at her long dark hair and all of her facial features, and then she looked hard into her eyes, wondering how they could change color. Maybe depending on her mood, maybe on her clothes, maybe the weather; she was not sure but she thought it was pretty cool. Then Jesus spoke to her and said, "I made you. You are exactly how I want you to be and if you are able to accept other people for how I made them, then why can you not accept you for how I made you?" Thank you, Jesus! Slowly, over the next few years, the confused adult began to shed worthlessness, doubt, self-denial, embarrassment, and self-hatred because she finally understood **just** how much Jesus loved her!

He is Not the Author of Confusion

...

Although I Corinthians 14:33 is talking about a disorderly type of confusion within the church, I believe that He is not the author of any type of confusion. He wants what is best for us and emotional confusion is not good for us. I Peter 5:7 tells us to cast "all your care upon Him, for He cares for you" (NKJV). Confusion in your mind is destructive to your physical well-being, just as confusion in the church is destructive to the church body.

If God is not the author of confusion, who is? Of course, you know the answer to that question, Satan. Even though we know this fact, it is still hard not to be confused by all of the emotional turmoil going on inside of our heads.

In the very first chapter of his book "The Be Happy Attitudes," of which

Robert Schuller titled "I need help - I can't do it alone!" He states that the first step to happiness is to admit that you need help. "Blessed are you when you face up to your emotional lack, admit your weakness. Blessed are you when you don't try to be an island and do it all by yourself." p. 11

It's tough to know where to start when you are confused. Your thoughts are already jumbled up and the process of thinking things through in a rational, concise manner is nearly impossible. That's where the great teaching of my Mom comes in . . . "Make a list." Yes, it can be as simple as that, at least it's a start. We are already confused by all the stuff in our past, then pile on top of that all of the responsibilities of today, tomorrow, next week, next month, this year, etc. It's no wonder we can't think clearly. So, "Make a list." Start with the immediate - what has to be done now? Then go on to future things. Keep this list handy, so you can refer to it daily, and make changes as things get completed or new things added.

Once you have that out of your head, go to the past. List all of the things that keep clouding your mind. What was said that you can't unsay? What did your family member, or friend, do or say to you that you keep dwelling on? What are things that you would change, but can't? Get it all out on paper. Then give it to Jesus and destroy the paper. There is no sense in keeping it around for you to read later and be reminded of all that garbage. Once it's under the blood, leave it there.

Remember: Cast all of your cares on Him for He cares for you!

He.

Cares.

For.

YOU!

Grasp it, hold it tight, and believe it!

<u>Notes</u>

7. The Blessed Little Girl

Once upon a time, there lived a very blessed little girl! She was blessed because she had a family and a wonderful Christian heritage. She was blessed because she grew up on a farm. She was blessed because Jesus came to live in her heart when she was eight years old. She was blessed because she had best friends who went to church with her. She was blessed because she had wonderful Sunday School teachers and pastors. She was blessed because she was never hungry, she had shelter, and she had clothes to wear.

The blessed little girl grew into a blessed teenager. As a teenager, she was blessed because she began to hear Jesus speak to her. She was blessed to be given spiritual dreams and visions. She was blessed because she felt God call her to missions.

The blessed teenager became a very blessed adult. She was blessed to go to college. She was blessed with jobs. She was blessed to go to New Zealand and work in the church. She was blessed to meet her husband and work with him in the church. But her greatest blessings are her son, Joshua, and her daughter, Natasha. They have brought so much love, joy, and pride to the blessed adult and her husband. The blessed adult is very thankful to our loving, Heavenly Father for His hand upon her life, the healing of the emotional turmoil she was in, and for the many blessings He has bestowed upon her.

Thank you, Jesus! I love you with all my heart! With love, the happy, confident, glad, calm, healed, loved, and very blessed little girl within this adult.

I'm so Blessed

•••

I have thought about this devotion for quite some time now and the first thing that pops into my head every time is the song by Cain:

> I'm so blessed, I'm so blessed
> Got this heartbeat in my chest
> It doesn't matter about the rest
> If I got You Lord, I'm so blessed

Songwriters: Jonathan Lindley Smith / Logan Cain / Madison Cain / Matthew Joseph West / Taylor Cain
I'm So Blessed lyrics © Capitol CMG Publishing, Essential Music Publishing

To be honest, this has been the hardest devotion to write. One would wonder why when you're reporting the goodness of God. The answer: How can I begin to tell of ALL the blessings our Savior, our Healer, our Father, The One and Only True God, The Creator, The

Alpha and Omega, The Almighty has bestowed upon insignificant little me!

I have thought about this devotion for several weeks. One day as I was meditating on His mercies, I realized that was the answer. No matter what we go through in life. No matter what sins we commit. No matter the disappointments, shame, guilt, or even hurts; His mercies are new every day. He's a loving Father, willing to forgive us of our transgressions. He created us to be exactly who and what He wanted. Yes, sometimes we allow life to twist and pull us into something else, but we are flexible and God can fix us and put us back on the right path, we just need to place our lives back into His hands and allow Him to do His work.

Whenever the enemy starts whispering in your ear that you're not good enough, or no one loves you, or you're a sinner and God can't forgive you; read Lamentations 3. Many times I have caught myself thinking in the way Lamentations begins: verse 3 "I am the only one He punishes," verse 5 "He attacked and surrounded me with hardships and trouble," verse 8 "Even when I shouted and prayed for help, he refused to listen." AND the big one, verse 14 "I am a joke to everyone - no one ever stops making fun of me." Verse 19 "Just thinking of my troubles and my lonely wandering make me miserable." HOWEVER, don't stop there because verse 21 states "Then I remember something that fills me with hope." verses 22-26 "The Lord's kindness never fails! If he had not been merciful, we would have been destroyed. 23 The Lord can always be trusted to show mercy each morning. 24 Deep in my heart I say, 'The Lord is all I need; I can depend on Him!' 25 The Lord is kind to everyone who trusts and obeys Him. 26 It is good to wait patiently for the Lord to save us." (CEV)

Be blessed!

Notes

_____

_____

_____

_____

_____

_____

_____

_____

_____

Epilogue

P salm 116 CEV

1 I love you, Lord! You answered my prayers.

2 You paid attention to me, and so I will pray to you as long as I live.

3 Death attacked from all sides, and I was captured by its painful chains. But when I was really hurting,

4 I prayed and said, "Lord, please don't let me die!"

5 You are kind, Lord, so good and merciful.

6 You protect ordinary people, and when I was helpless, you saved me

7 and treated me so kindly that I don't need to worry anymore.

8 You, Lord, have saved my life from death, my eyes from tears, my feet from stumbling.

9 Now I will walk at your side in this land of the living.

10 I was faithful to you when I was suffering,

11 though in my confusion I said, "I can't trust anyone!"

12 What must I give you, Lord, for being so good to me?

13 I will pour out an offering of wine to you, and I will pray in your name because you have saved me.

14 I will keep my promise to you when your people meet.

15 You are deeply concerned when one of your loyal people faces death.

16 I worship you, Lord, just as my mother did, and you have rescued me from the chains of death.

17 I will offer you a sacrifice to show how grateful I am, and I will pray.

18 I will keep my promise to you when your people

19 gather at your temple in Jerusalem. Shout praises to the Lord!

https://www.biblegateway.com/passage/?search=Psalm%201 16&version=CEV

Notes

_____

_____

About The Author

Danell Coleman

With roots digging deep in the fertile farmland of Ohio, Danell's adventurous spirit led her halfway across the world to New Zealand in 1992. There she met her husband while pursuing her passion for missions. Together they have cultivated a loving family, including two cherished adult children and a wonderful daughter-in-law. For over 30 years, she has nurtured young lives, from her own children to the kids she now works with as a substitute teacher. Her heart for service also blossoms through her involvement in local church ministry and music. Danell has a heart after God and longs to see people surrender their hearts to Him. Though her travels have taken her far, Danell remains firmly planted in central Ohio, with her faith deeply rooted in God.

Made in United States
Troutdale, OR
09/14/2024

22805083R00037